food

to die for!

This book is dedicated to:

My mother
    who would have been proud of me.

My husband Hossein
    who became proud of me.

Author's note:

These recipes were gleaned from restaurants, friends, television, books and conversations. Where possible I have given credit to those who passed them on, I apologize to those I can't remember. Every recipe, photographed in this book, was made by me on the day of shooting - usually within 30 minutes. No tricks were used such as colouring, hair spray or oil spray. All wine was real wine and enjoyed by all who were present on that particular day!

National Library of Canada
ISBN 0-9683893-0-9

Published by *Sophar So Good Productions*
c/o Claudette Dionne
260 de Maisonneuve West
Montreal, Canada H2X 1Y9

Distributed by *Hushion House Publishing*
36 Northline Road
Toronto, Ontario M4B 3E2
Tel.: (416) 285-6100 Fax: (416) 285-1777

Color separations *TriA Graphix*
Printing *Groupe Litho Graphique Inc.*

Author: Kim Soudavar
Photography: Maryse Raymond
Design: Horseman Cooke McBains

Copyright © Kim Soudavar 1998

SOPHAR SO GOOD PRODUCTIONS

contents

Acknowledgements	6
Foreword	8
Soups	15
Starters	29
Pasta and Pizza	61
Salads	79
Meat and Poultry	89
Fish	113
Vegetables	123
Desserts	139
Index	156

to die for!

Acknowledgements

I didn't just sit down and write this book. I was pushed and bullied and threatened by certain people *(mind you they would probably call it encouragement)*. They are:

Ana & José Gubert Gomes
>who also gave me the honour of co-hosting and catering their daughter's wedding, and lent me some lovely props for the photos, and hounded me to death to get on with this project.

Claudette Dionne and Olivier Schupp
>who were extremely persistent in their questioning of when the final product would be ready and would I consider doing it in French.

Martha Fruchet
>who was the person who started me on this cooking caper eight years ago and consequently led my life to take yet another unexpected and highly enjoyable turn.

Nicole Sharp, Karin Picquot, Rita Salomon, Peachoo Datwani, Maria José Montoro and her sister Mariam Martin Fraile
>all who have eaten with relish these recipes and whose enthusiasm was most encouraging. *(although I'm perfectly aware of the fact that it solves their entire Christmas present list even if it comes out in May).*

Olivier and Joan Leroy and Mati Gomes Mitchell
>for lending me some exquisite props for the photos.

Joaquina and Rosa
>who have chopped and cleaned and kept an eye on the stove during almost every lesson over the last 6 years - always with a smile.

The cooking students
>in particular **Roz Druckman, Pat** and **Joe Homa, Vera Hardy** and **Suzanne Laberge** who loyally kept coming back for more once they realized that things don't have to be complicated to be good and that the food is only an excuse for social interaction.

Roy McLaren
>who was called upon at the n'th hour to put all these recipes onto the computer, worked ceaselessly for 5 days and nights doing so, and only wanted six new reeds for his bag pipes as compensation and who I'm pretty sure never in his life expected to have his name in a cookbook.

Abolala Soudavar,
    my brother-in-law, for pointing out to Hossein that perhaps I wasn't just banging pots around in the kitchen and making a lot of noise and that maybe he should take another look at what I was doing.
    Lastly and mostly

Hossein Soudavar
    who innocently and unquestioningly subsidized eight years of my teaching, encouraged me to go to different schools in Europe to learn, took me to some extraordinary restaurants in the name of research and who finally had the nerve to announce during the arrangements for a move back to Europe that three photographers were coming to be interviewed in half an hour, and that I should make myself available as he wanted all the shooting done in our house before we moved. Nothing like working with a deadline - but he knew that was what it was going to take.

I THANK YOU ALL.

    Those physically involved in this *'masterpiece'* were:

Maryse Raymond
    whose photographs are extraordinary and who I know is proud of this project.

Gaston Adam
    my gentle and kind friend, who pillaged and plundered his own garden and who made me realize that I too could style a photo if I followed his delicate touch.

Gary Cooke
    my very talented friend who transformed my typed recipes and Maryse's photographs into this beautiful and stunning book. We met in Italy on a cooking course where we discovered that our mutual interests not only included food but also design, photography and humour.

Foreword

I have never read one, so I am not writing one. I think you will find the following tips much more useful.

Tips
Things you may or may not know.

Anchovies
A natural salt substitute. When heated they melt. Never mention them as so many people loathe them. What the eye cannot see you can get away with.

Apple cider vinegar
Less harsh than the wine ones. Good for everyday dressings with olive oil. It also has medicinal properties and can be taken for all sorts of complaints. I went through a period of having 1 tsp honey and 1 tsp apple cider vinegar in a cup of boiling water first thing in the morning and last thing at night. It's delicious *(but I cannot remember what I was suffering from and whether I improved).*

Artichokes
Two things.
1) There's a lady who sits in the open air market square in Verona and all she does is trim and take the choke out of artichokes. She then tosses them into a large pail of water that has parsley sprigs floating in it. Think of all the lemon juice we've been wasting for all these years.
2) Don't take the stems off. Just cut off ⅛" and scrape the stalk - it's the same as the heart and absolutely criminal to throw it away.

Asparagus
My friend Martha taught me that asparagus snaps at the tender point. So instead of cutting the tough part off, snap it and you'll be surprised how much more you'll get.

Balsamic vinegar
If you're cooking with it use the supermarket variety. If you're dressing with it get a better quality - more syrupy and less tart.

Baking
There are bakers and there are cooks. I am a cook so measurements don't have to be precise. However, when you bake you do have to measure exactly. Another thing - you never bake on the bottom oven shelf - always in the middle.

Burning a sauce
If you're making a sauce and you get distracted and realize it's burned, *DON'T* stir it. Just tip the unburned part into a clean pot and continue.

Carrots
If you're using carrots for *'garnish'*, by all means use those little designer ones. However, if you're using them for taste, texture and colour use the large mature ones - much more taste.

Cheese
A book in itself. However,

Parmigiano - don't buy it already grated. Buy a block and grate it as you need it or shave it with a vegetable peeler. There is nothing more delicious than a block of parmesan, grapes, crusty bread and red wine - so often people forget that this cheese is divine with or without pasta. It can be frozen. Remember never serve grated cheese with a shellfish sauce as in *'linguini alla vongole'* - serious culinary faux pas (*'bruta figura'*).

Brie - rather innocuous unless you buy *'lait cru'* - now we're talking.

Chevre - beat some of the soft type into your salad dressing and pour it over some perfect Boston lettuce leaves - too divine.

Roquefort, Danish Blue, Gorgonzola - all wonderful on their own and in sauces. *Entrecôte sauce Roquefort* and *Penne al Gorgonzola* cause my saliva glands to start spurting. I once had a peeled pear which had its core removed and filled with Roquefort and then sliced horizontally so that every slice had a cheese centre. It was wonderful.

Mozzarella - only buffalo milk mozzarella actually tastes and should be sliced and served with a few drops of fruity olive oil and ground pepper. The other type is for texture but can also be enhanced by having a few drops of pesto dribbled on top.

Stilton - please don't drown it with port. Serve it with a glass of port.

Feta - the Bulgarian type is less salty and creamier than the Greek type.

Coffee grounds
When you have made your filter coffee, keep some of the used grounds and put them in a small bowl by the sink. Wash your hands with some to remove onion, garlic and fish smells. Rinse. A miracle. Thank you Diana.

Consommé in tins
Put it in the fridge and serve it jellied with a dab of sour cream and chopped parsley - So chic and so painless.

Dogs dinner
⅓ cooked lean meat
⅓ cooked vegetables
⅓ cooked pasta or rice

Result

frightfully happy healthy creatures. How would you like to eat dry pellets for the rest of your life?

Dried Beans
When soaking overnight in water add a teaspoon of baking soda - all concerned will be extremely grateful - reduces flatulence.

Duck
I learned this in France. Put the duck into a *COLD* oven and turn the heat on. Much crispier skin!

Entertaining

Rule of thumb *KEEP IT SIMPLE*. The object of the exercise is to share a meal and exchange ideas. If you're doing it to impress, save your energy and go to a restaurant.

Menu deciding

Ask your guests what they *DON'T* eat. If they're frequently invited keep a card on them so you don't feel like an idiot by asking everytime. *(For your information I cannot abide cooked celery.)* Remember to 'balance', e.g. Don't serve a cream soup, followed by something in a cream sauce, followed by crème brulée. The result would be dinner guests dropping like flies.

Shopping list

When you've decided what you're going to serve write down all the ingredients in columns:
Meat   Vegetables   Dairy   Dry Goods   Wine   Bread   Flowers
(The last three never change). Amazingly simple and time saving.

Place seating

Don't put a good conversationalist next to a shy inhibited person. Put the live wire opposite another live wire in the middle of the table and before you know it everyone will be animated. Don't forget that if you are a guest your host/hostess has gone to some effort for your enjoyment, so rise to the occasion even if you don't feel great or have just had an argument. Better to cancel than ruin an evening.

Tone

You as a host set the tone by your mix of guests, your menu selection and your table setting.

Caterers

Essential for big gatherings. However try the main dish before you finalize the contract. The key here is *FLAVOUR*. All too often one is presented with a piece of meat that it is impossible to tell from which animal it came from. Keep in mind that the simpler the better. You really don't need soup, first course, sorbet, main course, salad, cheese, pudding and petit fours. This is definitely arriviste and not *'a good thing'*.

Eggs

If you beat them at room temperature you get 1/3 more volume.

Fennel and parsnip

Both incredibly underrated and delicious. Braised fennel and fennel salad are gifts from heaven.

Roast parsnips are to die for and boiled parsnip and carrot purée leave me speechless - Get the message?

Flush

Not feeling flush? Use Parmigiano Padano or Pecorino. Also use Pecorino as a savoury, sliced with poached, sliced and grilled pears. *OOH!!*

Green vegetables

If you want them to stay really green, boil or steam them *UNCOVERED*.

Herbs

As in parsley, basil, mint, dill, and chives. To keep them fresh put them in a vase with water and cover with a transparent plastic bag. Put it in the fridge. To save them *(because either you didn't use the whole bunch or you can't always find them)* put them in a food processor with olive oil and then keep them in a jar in the fridge.

Hot oil
If you put something into hot oil it will brown. If you put something into cold oil and then heat, it will cook but not brown.

Lobsters
When boiling them add a shot of vodka to the pot before you put them in. For some reason this makes them wonderfully tender.

Metric versus Imperial
Simplify your life and use metric. Why? In the metric system you have grams and kilos for weight and ml's and litres for volume. But in the Imperial system you have ounces for weight AND volume. Not everyone realizes that if 1 cup = 8 oz this is not a weight measurement - it is a volume. Example 1 cup of flour does not weigh the same as 1 cup of sugar, but they are both 8 oz of volume. Terribly confusing so just buy a metric scale and a metric jug and get on with it.

Mise en place
Once you get into the habit of pre-preparing all your ingredients you'll wonder why on earth you didn't cook like this before. I buy small bowls and do all my chopping, slicing, mincing etc. Put every ingredient into its own bowl, line them up in the order you're going to use them and start.

Olive oil
If you are cooking with it use a normal virgin oil - I like the Greek Calamata type. If you are dressing with it use 'first cold pressed virgin' - I like the ones from Spain and Portugal. *(Did you know that Italy does not have enough olive oil for its own need so much is mixed with Greek olive oil).*

Oregano
I use the dried from Greece.

Oranges and lemons
Always choose the thin skinned ones - you get much more juice.

Pasta
Not too simple to do well, unless you follow some ground rules. The biggest mistake is OVERCOOKING. When you watch an Italian housewife cook pasta, the first thing she does is look at the number of minutes cooking time suggested by the manufacturer. This is very important information but totally ignored by the rest of the world. The next thing is that the water must be salted and boiling before the pasta is tipped in. *AND YOU MUST STIR* the pasta. The stirring is what keeps it from sticking, not a waste of your precious olive oil.

The pasta must be served onto hot plates, so put the plates in the sink and drain the pasta through a sieve onto them. Put the drained pasta into the sauce, toss gently, wipe the plates (careful they're very hot) and serve immediately. Please remember *NOT* to put the sauce onto the pasta, the pasta goes *INTO* the sauce.

So the sequence is:
1) Make sauce in large pot.
2) Boil lots of salted water.
3) Read suggested cooking time.
4) Add pasta to boiling water and *STIR*. *(continued overleaf)*

5) Drain pasta over plates in the sink.
6) Gently mix the pasta into the sauce.
7) Wipe plates and serve immediately.

Committing this to memory will change your life! Oh and by the way, serving grated cheese with any fish or shellfish as in Vongole is such a no no that you'll be lucky not to be ostracised from society and feel everyone talking behind their hands to each other muttering in shocked and scandalous tones: *"My dear she served cheese with the vongole! Tsk Tsk. Whatever next!"*

Potatoes

In France they've got umpteen varieties - for specific uses. I basically use Idaho for roasting, frying and mashing; red ones for salad; new ones for boiling *(add butter and mint to accompany fish);* yellow ones for stews.

Rapini/Broccoli rabe

Forget the mundane brocolli which almost always disintegrates. Steam some rapini and dress with lemon juice, olive oil and salt. *OOH OOH OOH!*

Recipes

You can probably be sure that generosity of spirit is not one of the qualities of someone who will not share a recipe. You have been warned. Remember in life we get hit with a pebble before we get hit with a brick.

Reducing

When the recipe says reduce by half - stick a wooden chopstick in as a measuring aid. You can easily see the amount reduced.

Re-inventing the wheel

Don't waste your time . Life is too short. Buy puff pastry. Use stock cubes or cans. Buy frozen berries for coulis, Bisto for gravy and won ton skins for ravioli - *SIMPLIFY.*

Rice

There are only two kinds worth knowing:
Arborio for risotto,
Basmati for everything else.

Salad

To keep salad leaves crisp and fresh, wash them, dry them and put them in a plastic bag, but *DON'T* squeeze the air out. The more air around the leaves the less chance of contamination.

Salt

Too much in the soup? Put in a whole, peeled raw potato. Don't use a lot of salt, let everyone add their own as it really is a matter of taste.

Sauté

Just a chic word for fry.

Small talk

My personal nightmare. Just remember most people love to talk about themselves.

Stirring

Stop fiddling with the food. How can it possibly cook if you keep moving and turning and patting it?

Stock

The days of roasting bones and then simmering them with meat and vegetables have gone the same way as the black and white TV. We now have Knorr cubes - chicken, beef, veal, fish and vegetables. We also have tins of bouillon. *Note:* Consommé is *NOT* bouillon.

Tomatoes

I've never seen the point of a pink tomato. They should be firm and red. Italian plum tomatoes don't really taste until they've been heated e.g. boiled for a pasta sauce or roasted with garlic and oil. Canned whole peeled Italian tomatoes are a must in Italian cooking and sometimes the tins of chopped ones are good. I prefer the cartons of those made by Parmalat.

soups

French Onion Soup	17
Lentil Soup	18
Vichyssoise	19
Sbollichini	21
Persian Yoghurt Soup	23
Gazpacho	25
Cold Borscht	27

to die for!

French Onion Soup

My parents first took me to Paris when I was five years old on our way back to England from Malaya. To say the least the culture shock was extreme *(I had left England at the age of ten months)* and I was always cold, but a bowl of French onion soup seemed to do the trick. It took me years and many recipes to come up with something that satisfied my memories. *This one also seems to satisfy everyone else's!*

Peel
4 large Spanish onions,
slice them thinly *(I use a mandolin)* and slowly sauté them in
butter or oil
or a combination of both over a low heat until they are soft BUT NOT BROWN.
This takes about 30 minutes.
When they are limp sprinkle them with
50 g/2 oz flour
and gently mix with a spatula.
Add:
500 ml/2 cups of white wine
and enough
tinned beef or chicken bouillon
to cover by 1".
Simmer for 30 minutes.
Serve with a mixture of:
gruyère grated
and
parmesan cheese grated
and
baguette slices toasted.

tips:

- This can be frozen.

- Beef or chicken stock can be cubes or tins.

- If more people than you expected show up just add more stock and toast more croutons.

note:

Traditionally this dish is served in a small deep bowl with croutons and masses of melted cheese on top but I always feel there should be a pair of scissors on the table to help you cut the strands of hot cheese that are burning your lips. Apart from the pain it's also rather an unattractive sight. So make life simpler by serving it in a normal soup plate with melted cheese crouton on the side or with toast rounds and a bowl of grated cheese.

Lentil Soup

If I were ever put in a position where I could only have two cookbooks there is no doubt in my mind that they would be Marcella Hazan's *Italian Cooking Volumes 1 and 2*. My paperback copies are spattered and dog-eared and go with me wherever I go. I don't think you can improve on anything she cooks. She's the Bible. I trust she won't mind me passing this one on to you.

Sauté
2 tbs of onions chopped
    until golden in
3 tbs olive oil
    and
3 tbs butter.
    Add
4 tbs carrots finely chopped
    and continue to cook for 2-3 minutes.
    Add
75 g / 4 oz pancetta chopped
    (or prociutto or bacon),
    sauté 1 minute.
    Add:
250 ml / 1 cup tinned Italian tomatoes chopped,
    including the juice,
    and simmer for 25 minutes uncovered.
    Add
250 g / ½ lb dried lentils
    washed and drained.
    Stir and turn 2-3 times.
    Add:
1 litre / 4 cups of meat bouillon
    (or 1 cup canned beef bouillon and
    3 cups of water),
salt and pepper.
    Cover and gently simmer until lentils
    are tender.
    When done take off the heat, swirl in
1 tbs of butter
    and
3 tbs of parmesan freshly grated.

Eat and swoon with pleasure.

Vichyssoise

When I tasted Vichyssoise for the first time I thought I'd died and gone to heaven. Not in a million years did I think that it could be so easy to make.

Sauté
1 kg / 2 lbs leeks chopped
and
500 g / 1 lb potatoes cut into chunks
for approximately 8 minutes.
Add:
600 ml / 2½ cups chicken stock,
600 ml / 2½ cups of milk,
salt and pepper,
and
½ tsp of sugar.
Bring to the boil, lower the heat and simmer until soft.
Blend in a food processor or a blender, cool and chill.
Before serving thin the purée with
milk or light cream
or a combination of both.

Dress with chopped chives.

Sbollichini

Diana and Vic Folonari are friends of mine. I met them when I took her cooking course at their home in Positano on the Amalfi Coast. Her courses are held on the terrace overlooking the Mediterranean and while she attempts to convert the faint hearted to *'lotsa garlic'* and *'lotsa olive oil'*, Vic has no trouble converting everyone to his family's wines. Diana and I instantly took to each other; we both like dogs, wine and cigarettes and share the same sense of humour, so when I asked her to come to Montreal and give a series of courses with my students she enthusiastically accepted. And what a wonderful time was had by all. She is remembered by everyone who took her lessons, not only for her recipes but also for her gravelly voice, throaty laugh and no nonsense way of looking at life. *I adore her.*

Shell
1 kg / 2 lbs cranberry beans, *(also known as Romano beans).*
Put in a large pot.
Add:
10-12 garlic cloves
cut into chunks,
125 ml / ½ cup of olive oil,
water
to cover beans,
500 g / 1 lb fresh Italian plum tomatoes
cut into chunks,
1 tbs oregano dried,
handful of basil leaves torn.
Bring to the boil, lower heat, cover and simmer until done.

Serve in bowls and drizzle with a good fruity olive oil and grated parmesan.

Persian Yoghurt Soup

In August 1980 Hossein asked me to stay at his home in Marbella, Spain. I hadn't been back to Spain in about ten years and in addition to the fact that I rather more than liked him I accepted his invitation. When I arrived his sister and her two sons were there and unbeknownst to me they knew something that I didn't. The nephews taught me backgammon and his sister suggested one day that we go to the market to buy the ingredients for a cold Persian yoghurt soup. Off we trotted *(or at least I trotted behind her)* and purchased all the ingredients without any problem until we came to the 'dill'. I had left Spain when I was ten and consequently did not know the word in Spanish. The more I tried to explain to the stall vendors what I wanted, the more confused they became and the more irritated my future sister-in-law became. I grew increasingly nervous and so was very relieved when she pointed to some greenery and announced confidently that there indeed was the dill. She asked me to buy it but I refused. She insisted and I still refused. Finally she got quite cross and demanded to know why. My response was, *"Because there's a bunch of carrots attached to that greenery".*

This is one of my most successful recipes and a great way to start a summer meal. It's also *very good* the next day.

In a bowl mix:
1 cucumber peeled, seeded and diced,
100 g / 4 oz yellow raisins,
750 ml / 3 cups plain yoghurt,
125 ml / ½ cup sour cream,
50 g / 2 oz scallions chopped,
1 tbs mint chopped,
2 tbs dill chopped,
2 cloves garlic chopped,
3 tbs walnuts chopped,
1 tsp salt.
Add water until you have the texture that you like - not too thick, not too thin.

Chill and just before serving add some ice cubes.

Virginia's Gazpacho

Virginia is the wife of the gardener that we had in Spain during the first few years of our married life and she 'did' for us a few days a week. I would ask her to show me her version of my favourites and this is her gazpacho. You should be aware that there are as many recipes for gazpacho in Spain as there are women. You should also know that gazpacho *NEVER* has tomato juice in it. The amount of olive oil and vinegar is dependant on your taste so just keep sampling until you get it right. Don't be frightened. A glass of this is a wonderful way to start a summer meal.

Soak
4-6 slices of white sandwich bread
in water *(in Spain it's appropriately called Bimbo).* The bread should be sodden, not swimming.
Add in layers:
1 cucumber peeled and sliced,
5 ripe tomatoes chopped,
1 green pepper chopped,
2-3 garlic cloves chopped,
olive oil,
apple cider vinegar,
salt,
water.

Mix with an electric wand.
Taste and adjust seasoning.
Pass through a sieve pushing down on the pulp with the back of a ladle. Chill.

Serve with chopped tomatoes, chopped cucumber, chopped green pepper and croutons fried in olive oil.

options:

There are three textures for this recipe:

- **If you like thin soup you would pass it all through the sieve.**

- **For a sophisticated touch add a swirl of cream.**

- **I prefer $2/3$ of the mix sieved and the remaining $1/3$ just added and mixed in - more peasanty and thicker.**

Cold Borscht

During the last three years I've given cooking demonstrations for the Combined Jewish Appeal fund raising drive and when I give a class for these ladies I love to start with this recipe. I see them change from looking highly suspect at the beginning to sheer amazement when they taste the result. Then I know I've got their attention! Works every time.

Boil
8-10 medium beetroots
with the skin on until tender.
Drain but keep
250 ml / 1 cup of the purple water.
Peel the beetroots by simply twisting them in your hand.
(I wear plastic gloves).
Chill the beets and the reserved juice.
In a food processor put the chilled cut-up beets.
Add:
500 g / 1 lb of sour cream
and
1½ cans of chilled beef bouillon.
(1 can = 284 ml/10 fl oz)
Process until smooth and chill again.

Serve with tiny cubes of cucumber and finely sliced radish for a bit of a crunch.

tips:

- **If when serving more liquid is needed, add some of the reserved beet water.**

- **For a touch of sophistication add a dollop or swirl of cream.**

starters

Spanish Omelette	31
Red pepper, Tomato & Chevre Plate	33
Involtini di Peperoni *(Margherita)*	35
Onion Pie *(Margherita)*	37
Brewster's Bean Salad	38
Leeks Vinaigrette	39
Eggplant with Basil	41
Squid Salad	43
Olivier's Mackerel Paté	44
Skate with Coriander Vinaigrette	45
Salade Muscovite *(Wally)*	47
Scallop and Salmon Salad	49
Oeufs en Meurette	51
Vitello Tonnato	53
Thai Steak and Green Bean Salad	55
Frisée aux Lardons	56
Paté de Foies de Volaille *(Louise)*	59

to die for!

Spanish Omelette

Traditionally this thick omelette is cut into squares and a toothpick is inserted into each square. It is always present in a Tapas bar in Spain and is truly one of the most delicious things you can eat with a glass of sherry or wine.

Peel, slice or cube
4 potatoes
and fry in a lot of
olive oil.
When soft but not browned, drain.
Use some of the same oil to sauté
a small onion finely sliced.
Drain.
Add to the potatoes.
Mix in a bowl
4-6 eggs
with a fork and add to the potato/onion mixture.
Sauté all in a small frying pan.
When the underneath is brown, *(use a spatula to lift and peek underneath)*, place a plate upside down on top of the omelette and turn the whole thing over onto the plate. Put the pan back on the heat and slowly and carefully slide the omelette, brown-side up back into the pan.
Continue cooking until brown.

When done slip it straight onto a serving dish and serve at room temperature.

tips:

- **The more eggs you use, the fatter the omelette.**

- **Sherry must always be served chilled in a tulip shaped glass.**

Red Pepper, Tomato and Chevre Plate

Everytime I am in London I'm inevitably dashing from one part of town to another by tube, bus, cab or foot. My spirits begin to flag usually at around 3.30. p.m. and I always try to be near Conrans in the Michelin Building as the Oyster Bar at the entrance level is always open and serves wonderful light salads.

One of my favourites is the following and I serve it often at home with huge success - *and it's easy.*

Preheat oven to 200°C/400°F.

On a non-stick baking tray, place enough
red peppers (²/₃ pepper per person).
On the same tray lay
1 Italian tomato per person,
sliced lengthwise, cut side up.
Roast, constantly turning the peppers and making sure that the tomatoes do not burn.
Remove from the oven, cool, skin the peppers and tear each into 3 sections, remove the seeds.
Lay the pieces on a clean baking sheet and put
a dollop of soft chevre
in the middle.
Cover the chevre with the roast tomato and put into the oven until cheese melts.
Put on a serving plate and dribble with good fruity
olive oil,
a drop of balsamic vinegar
and
freshly ground pepper.

tip:

- When red peppers are in season and prices are at their lowest I buy them by the bushel, roast them, skin them and lay them flat on top of each other in plastic freezer bags. I forfeit one entire evening but I have wonderful peppers at a good price all year.

options:

- If you've got the time, grill thinly sliced eggplant and serve the red pepper on this.

- If you haven't got the time but you do have some Romaine lettuce, lay the pepper/cheese/tomato in the middle of each Romaine leaf - it makes an attractive presentation and adds some crunch.

Involtini di Peperoni *(Margherita)*

In the Spring of '96 we rented a house in Saló on the shore of Lago di Garda from a friend of ours, Lennart Pihl. I drove a few days ahead with Kiki, the niece of friends who was spending a few months helping me *(the Bassets are a lot of work)*, in order to set up house and discover everything about the town. Lennart was still there and the first evening asked me to join him and a couple he knew for dinner at a restaurant in the hills. The meal was memorable but more importantly Margherita and Jason came into our lives. We all had a passion for food and by the end of the meal I had persuaded Margherita to teach me some of her favourite recipes a couple of times a week. The two following recipes are from her repertoire and are absolutely delicious.

Preheat oven 230°C/450°F.

Place
8 red peppers
on a baking sheet and put them in the oven, turning every 5 minutes until the skin has loosened. Cool, skin, de-seed and tear each pepper into three strips.
Dice
4 slices of bread
into small cubes.
Sauté in
olive oil:
2 cloves of garlic chopped,
the bread cubes,
handful small black olives,
pitted and chopped,
handful of yellow raisins,
handful of pine nuts,
1 heaped tbs of capers.
After 5 minutes and constant stirring, cool.
Season with
salt and pepper.
Fill each pepper strip with the stuffing. Roll and place on the serving dish. Sprinkle each pepper with
basil chopped
and fruity
olive oil
and a drop of
balsamic vinegar.

note:

- Buy the longer peppers so you have enough to roll, not the short fat ones.
- You will probably have too much stuffing left over.

So you have-

2 options:

- Sprinkle the remainder on top of the peppers.
- Eat the remainder straight from the pan when nobody is looking.

Onion Pie *(Margherita)*

This is wonderful for a buffet or as a first course or as a lunch dish with a simple green salad.

The night before
defrost frozen commercial
puff pastry,
enough for the top and bottom of the pie.
Preheat oven 200°C/400°F.
Finely slice
2 Kg / 4 lb of onions.
Sauté in a little
olive oil.
Cover until soft *BUT NOT* coloured.
Add water if neccessary.
When soft add:
1 handful black olives
pitted and chopped,
200 g / 6½ oz ricotta *drained,*
100 g / 3¼ oz parmesan *freshly grated.*
Mix gently.
Roll half the puff pastry
to fit bottom and sides of a
9" buttered cake tin,
leaving the edges hanging.
Fill with the onion mix. Season with
salt and pepper.
Roll the other half of the puff pastry,
cover the pie, pinch around the edge,
and prick the surface with a fork.
Brush with
1 egg *beaten.*
Bake for 30 minutes until golden.

tips:

- **Slice the onions on a mandolin.**

- **Drain the ricotta for 10 minutes (while you're crying over the onions).**

Brewster's Bean Salad

Brewster is an American friend of ours who lives in Spain and who is passionate about cooking. He showed me this dish one day and a few years later I served it to him as part of an antipasto plate. He raved about it and asked me for the recipe!

Open and drain
1-2 tins of red kidney beans.
Wash gently. Drain and tip into the serving bowl.
Chop
1 onion
and quite a bit of
Italian parsley
and add to the beans.
Add
salt
to taste.

vinaigrette:

dijon mustard,
apple cider vinegar,
and
olive oil.
Pour over the beans, toss and chill.

Better if assembled a couple of hours before eating.

Leeks Vinaigrette

This is a standard French hors d'oeuvre and you should note that the finer the leeks the younger they are and therefore more tender than those huge fat ones. If you want to dress this dish up a bit just add chopped boiled egg and parsley to the vinaigrette and spoon over the leeks. *You* decide how many leeks per person.

Trim the
leeks
and cut them lengthwise almost to the root and wash them well.
(There's nothing worse than gritty leeks).
Tie 4 in a bundle with
kitchen string
to stop them falling apart and simmer gently in water until very tender
(this takes longer than you think).
Drain and cool.

vinaigrette:

dijon mustard,
vinegar,
olive oil.
Pour it gently over the leeks.

Eggplant with Basil

You'll never be able to make enough of this - it's so delicious.

    Slice
eggplants
    thinly, lengthwise.
    Arrange in a layer on a plate or tray.
    Sprinkle with
salt
    and cover with paper towel.
    Repeat until all slices are salted.
    Leave for ½ hour.
    With a paper towel dry each slice.
    With a pastry brush, paint each slice with
olive oil
    and either grill, fry or broil until done.
    As they are done, place 1 layer in a serving dish,
    and sprinkle with
basil torn
    and
1 tbs balsamic vinegar/olive oil vinaigrette.
    Repeat until all the slices are layered.

    Serve at room temperature.

tips:

- **When slicing eggplant I find it relatively easy if you slice off both ends. Stand the eggplant on its fat end and turn it until you see a straight vertical edge. Start slicing down from that point. Use a long, sharp knife.**

- **Sauté some cut up red peppers in olive oil and dress with the same olive oil/balsamic vinegar vinaigrette. Also wonderful.**

Squid Salad

Without a doubt Milos, a Greek restaurant in Montreal, serves the most consistently good, simple, fresh food I have eaten in North America. The downside is that you leave most of your inheritance there when you pay the bill. However, this recipe is a delicious way to serve not only squid but also octopus, red peppers and shitake mushrooms. Don't forget to serve them with doorstep size slices of grilled country bread to mop up the juices.

Wash
squid
and take out the insides.
Dry.
Brush with
olive oil
and grill until golden.
Cut into circles.
Sprinkle with:
onions *finely sliced,*
red wine vinegar,
olive oil,
parsley *chopped,*
capers.

Serve warm with lemons cut in half.

comment:

- There is nothing more irritating than lemon slices. You can't squeeze them, you can't eat them, all you can do is mush them. So please cut the lemons into halves or quarters. Thank you.

Olivier's Mackerel Paté

Olivier Schupp is a big gentle giant and a very good friend of mine. He is a sculptor and a stone mason and his passion is cooking, hence we can spend considerable time together in the kitchen jointly preparing a dinner for 8 or 20 people. His mother lives in St Malo and whilst visiting her a couple of years ago he discovered fish rillette. I love this recipe and you can do it with any fish - *I particularily like it with mackerel.*

Chop off the head and tail of a
good sized mackerel
(or 2 small ones)
and cut into 2" pieces.
In a pot put:
water,
salt and pepper,
1 garlic clove peeled,
1 onion or 2 shallots peeled,
peppercorns,
parsley.
Boil and add mackerel, lower heat and cook 10 -15 minutes until done.
In a bowl mix:
1 egg yolk,
juice of 1 lime,
chives chopped,
3 shallots chopped,
salt and pepper,
thyme leaves or fines herbes,
pinch of cayenne,
2 tbs dijon mustard.
To this add a touch of
liquid cream or **crème fraîche.**
Skin and de-bone the fish.
Break it up with a fork and bit by bit add it into the sauce.

Serve with toasted or baked baguette slices.

Skate with Coriander Vinaigrette

I've noticed that skate is in the same category as snails and artichokes when it comes to knowing how to eat something. This recipe takes all the fear away as it's taken off the bone. Even people who aren't particularly fond of fish seem to come back for seconds of this dish.

Vinaigrette:
dijon mustard,
sherry vinegar,
olive oil,
½ small red onion chopped,
capers,
scallion sliced,
1 tsp coriander seeds heated and crushed, (optional).

Skate:
Have the *skate wing(s)* skinned.
Place in skillet, cover with:
cold water,
1 onion sliced,
2 tbs white vinegar,
dash of white wine,
2 parsley sprigs.
Bring to boil, lower and simmer for 15 minutes.
Remove from bone and spoon the vinaigrette over the fish.

Serve immediately while warm.

notes:

- **Skate is also known as ray.**

- **The bones are not bones, they are cartilage.**

Salade Muscovite *(Wally)*

I have an actress friend in Paris with flaming red hair, incredible blue eyes, a Russian temper and French charm. Her name is Wally and she made this recipe the first time she invited us for dinner and followed it with pot au feu and a chocolate bar. It was wonderful. This recipe is a clear winner amongst my students.

Put into a bowl:
2 cucumbers peeled, halved, de-seeded and finely sliced,
1 black radish finely sliced,
(or 6 red radishes finely sliced),
2 tbs thick cream,
1½ tbs poppy seeds,
salt,
basil leaves torn,
sprinkling of paprika,
smoked salmon diced and marinated in
juice of a lemon.
Mix gently.

note:

- The quantity of smoked salmon depends on you. If you're feeling flush then 3 slices diced per person is good, if not 1 slice per person is also good.

Scallop and Salmon Salad

This is such a lovely dish and if you do your *mise en place* it takes only about 7 minutes. I often serve it for lunch on the weekends followed by cheese and fresh fruit.

Cut into julienne:
carrots,
leeks,
red peppers,
and sauté in
olive oil.
Make a
vinaigrette *(dijon mustard, vinegar and olive oil)*
and warm it in a small pot.
Sauté in
hot olive oil
some
fresh salmon *cubed*
and
scallops *sliced in half horizontally.*
Tear some
frizzy lettuce or Boston lettuce
and arrange on a plate.
Cover with fish, scallops and vegetables.

Drizzle with the warm vinaigrette.

options:

- Use any fish and shell fish - it's your taste. It could just as well be done with cubed halibut and shrimps.

- If you don't have leeks use spring onions.

- You decide on the quantities. You know how much fish and vegetables you can eat, so just multiply it by however many people you're cooking for.

Oeufs en Meurette

For the last 12 years on the day that I arrive in Paris my first meal is always at the restaurant around the corner 'La Fontaine de Mars' on the Rue St Dominique. I love the food and adore the owners and staff. For years, especially at lunchtime and particularily in winter, I would see patrons digging into a baked dish with an egg on top. Being curious I eventually asked what it was, ordered it, devoured it, asked for a few hints on how to make it and VOILÀ, here you are. Incidentally, since that first tasting I have never had any other first course - *why change a good thing?*

Preheat oven 175°C/350°F.

Cut
1 slice of lardons *per person*
into strips. Blanche, in boiling water for one minute, drain and sauté in
butter
until golden.
Drain on paper towel.
Sauté
onions chopped
in
butter.
Add the cooked lardons and
2-3 tbs flour,
500 ml / 2 cups red wine,
or a mixture of wine and
beef or chicken stock,
salt and pepper.
Reduce by ⅓ until slightly thickened.
Put sauce in individual dishes, break an
egg
on top of each.
Bake until desired 'doneness' of egg.

Serve with triangles of fried bread.

tip:

● **Sauce can be made way ahead and reheated.**

Vitello Tonnato

I met Vitello Tonnato when I was in my mid thirties and as far as I'm concerned that was about 25 years too late. It's one of my favourite dishes and you'd be surprised how many people haven't eaten it. I strongly advise you *not* to describe it as sliced veal with a tuna sauce - just wait until they've tried it.

Veal:

1.5 kg / 3 lbs veal roast *rolled and tied.*
3 flat anchovies *cut into 1" pieces.*
1-2 garlic cloves *sliced.*

    Put anchovies and garlic slithers into veal.
    Immerse in a pot of cold water, bring to the boil for 1 minute.
    Take it out and rinse the scum off.
    Put the roast into a clean pot with:

1 litre / 4 cups chicken stock,
500 ml / 2 cups white wine,
500 ml / 2 cups water,
2 onions *quartered,*
2 carrots *chopped,*
2 bay leaves,
6 parsley sprigs,
10 pepper corns.

    Bring to boil, reduce heat, simmer for 1½ hrs.
    Cool in its own stock.
    Save ½ cup stock in a small bowl.
    Freeze the rest for a soup base.

Sauce:

    In a food processor whizz:
175 ml / ¾ cup olive oil,
1 egg yolk,
1 can Italian tuna,
4 flat anchovies,
2 tbs lemon juice.

    Transfer to a bowl.
    Slowly add
60 ml / ½ cup cream or **yoghurt**
    and
60-120 ml / ¼ - ½ cup strained stock
    and
1 tbs capers.
    Stir gently.

Slice veal very thinly, cover with sauce and garnish with thin lemon slices. (These are only to make the dish look pretty)!

tips:

- You can always make the sauce go further by adding more stock **NOT** cream.

- The stock left over from the veal cooking is one of the most delicious you will ever taste so whatever you do **DON'T** throw it away, just strain it and freeze it.

Thai Steak and Green Bean Salad

This dish is on almost every menu in a Thai restaurant. I've seen it done with ground meat but I personally prefer it with steak strips. It's extremely refreshing and a great success.

Dressing:

Mince and mash
2 garlic cloves
with
½ tsp salt.
In a bowl mix:
125 ml / ½ cup fresh lime juice,
3 tbs soy sauce,
1 tbs sugar,
2 x 4" fresh hot chillies,
seeded and thinly sliced (wash your hands immediately afterwards),
handful of fresh mint thinly sliced,
and the garlic and salt paste.
Leave at least 30 minutes.

Salad:

Sprinkle
500 g / 1 lb sirloin or flank steak
(1½" thick)
with
black pepper freshly ground.
Brush with
vegetable oil.
Grill or sauté over high heat.
When done put it on a rack placed on a plate and let settle for 15 minutes.
In a pan heat ½" oil until almost smoking and fry
8 shallots thinly sliced,
until golden.
Drain on paper and reserve.
Trim and cut diagonally.
375 g / ¾ lb green beans
and cook UNCOVERED in salted boiling water until crisp and tender. Reserve.
Rinse and trim
100 g / 4 oz fresh bean sprouts.
Cut the steak into ½" thick slices.
Mix with: green beans,
sprouts,
shallots
and toss with the prepared dressing.

tips:

- Roll the limes and press down on them before you squeeze them - you'll get more juice.

- Add the steak juice to the dressing.

Frisée aux Lardons

A few years ago during a truly awful Montreal winter a group of us would meet every Saturday for a long relaxed lunch at Chez Gauthier, a French bistro. Every Saturday that I was there my lunch was soupe de poisson followed by frisée aux lardons accompanied by lashings of red wine and followed by a three hour siesta. A perfect antidote to slush and -20°C.

During the summer when we always had open house for Sunday lunch - the only rule being that you had to phone by Saturday 6pm to say if you were coming so I had a vague idea of numbers - I decided this would be rather a good dish for the die hards who were still there at 7pm. I didn't really know what lardons were but I knew it was pork so I went down to the 'Main' *(St Lawrence Blvd)* where there were many Eastern European butcher shops that specialized in pork cuts and sausages. In one of them I encountered a very stout woman with a very unwelcoming gaze in a white overall standing with arms akimbo behind the counter. Feeling less than confident I launched into a description of what I was looking for which must have taken a full two minutes. When I was finished she looked me straight in the eye and said "So how much slab bacon you vont?"
A humbling experience.

Rinse, spin and tear into pieces
frisée or chicory lettuce.
Cut thick slices of
smoked lardon
(also called smoked slab bacon)
into small pieces and sauté until crisp.
Drain.
Make a traditional vinaigrette:
dijon mustard,
vinegar,
olive oil
and warm these three in a pot.
Bring a pot of water to the boil and with care slip in
one raw egg *(per person).*
Turn constantly with a spoon and when ready, drain and keep warm.
Place the salad in a bowl, dress, toss in the lardons with much enthusiasm and gay abandon as lunch is on its way.

Place the salad on individual plates and top with the poached egg.

tips:

- **This makes a very nice quick lunch and the bonus is that for some inexplicable reason, children like it.**

- **You can also use chicken livers instead of lardons.**

Paté de Foies de Volaille *(Louise)*

A few years ago we were invited to dinner at Louise and Gerald Van de Werve's house. We didn't know them very well so we were looking forward to some new ideas and exchanges and we were not in the least disappointed. The company was stimulating *(we hadn't met any of the other guests),* the dining room was long and had french doors leading into the garden and the food was sublime and casual - just up my alley. We started with this paté and watercress salad followed by navarin d'agneau, cheese and dessert. The conversation was animated, the room was warm, the snow was bucketing down outside and I was happy as a clam. I'll never forget it. This is a marvellous first course - don't expect to have any left.

Trim
500 g / 1 lb of fresh chicken livers.
Put in a bowl:
2 thyme sprigs,
1 bay leaf,
the chicken livers,
salt and pepper,
Port
(enough to submerge and surround the livers).
Leave 2-3 hours.
Later on chop
1 onion.
In a frying pan cook the livers, Port and onion for about 20 minutes or until soft and done.
Remove the bay leaf and thyme.
Tip everything into a food processor and add
125 g / 4 oz of butter cut into cubes.
Put into a serving dish, chill.

Serve with a simple water cress salad and toasted country bread.

pasta & pizza

Penne al Gorgonzola	63
Linguine alle Vongole	65
Pesto *(My Bastardisation)*	67
Pasta and Eggplant Timbalo	69
Bruno's Pasta	70
Spaghetti alla Checca *(Keka)*	71
Aspen Pastini *(Ajax Tavern)*	73
Rissotto 4 Fromaggi	75
Pizzas	77

to die for!

Penne al Gorgonzola

When Diana Folonari took over my school for 10 days this recipe definitely won in the Pasta section. This was amazing as North Americans are so fat conscious that we feared there would be no takers but when we pointed out that one wouldn't serve it daily, the students became braver. There was none left for Diana or myself ! *This is my favourite sauce.*

Blend in a pot over low heat:
125 g / 4 oz butter,
250 g / 8 oz gorgonzola,
½ cup parmesan freshly grated,
fresh sage leaves,
cream (or milk / cream mix),
salt and pepper.
Stir until thick, keep warm.
Cook penne (rigate) al dente.
Drain and stir into the sauce.
Cook another 2-3 minutes.
Serve *IMMEDIATELY*.

tips:

- **Don't leave out the sage - make an effort and find some.**

- **You can't imagine how fast the pasta absorbs this sauce so please serve it fast and immediately.**

- **You'll notice there's no quantity for the cream. That's because as the sauce heats it becomes thicker so you keep adding a bit more until you get the consistency *YOU* require.**

Linguine alle Vongole

This is so easy and so good. For goodness sakes don't turn your nose up at tinned clams, they're delicious, grit free and there are masses of them in each tin.

Heat some
olive oil
in a frying pan.
Add and continually stir together
3 cloves of garlic chopped,
freshly ground black pepper,
½ handful of Italian parsley coarsely chopped,
125 ml / ½ cup of white wine.
Cook for one minute and add
1 tin of clams drained,
but save the juice.
Sizzle off some of the wine fumes and add some of the
clam juice.
Cook for 2 minutes and add
250 g / 8 oz fresh tomatoes diced.
Cook 5 minutes and add more
fresh parsley coarsely chopped.
Tip the cooked, drained pasta into this delicious sauce.

notes:

- I keep the clam juice in a bowl and add it as I need it.

- If you want to dress this up buy a few fresh clams, add them to the sauce, cover and steam until they're open, ladle some juice over them and decorate each plate with 2 or 3.

- Cheese is never served with a fish sauce.

Pesto *(my bastardization)*

Fifteen years ago I'd never had pesto and all of a sudden it became the fashion. So I mixed what I thought was in it and this is what I came up with, and very successfully I might add. It never occurred to me that there were supposed to be pine nuts in it. My version is much lighter.

Put into a food processor:
handful of fresh basil leaves,
2-3 garlic cloves peeled,
1 tsp tomato paste.
Turn the machine on and add a stream of
olive oil.
Tip this into a serving bowl.
Cook and drain
pasta,
(I use spaghettini).
Tip into the bowl with the Pesto and toss.

Serve with cherry tomatoes cut in half and sautéed in butter and freshly grated parmesan.

notes:

● **Buy tomato paste in a tube - there's no waste.**

● **Store this sauce in a jar in the fridge for emergencies.**

● **When you serve sliced tomatoes and mozzarella add a few drops of this on the cheese and you'll find it perks up the palate.**

Pasta and Eggplant Timbalo

The best way to treat this dish is to put aside about 3 hours, make 4 of them and freeze however many you don't need. It is so impressive and so good that you forget how much time you spent on it when you soak up the praise. Put them together in any size *Pyrex* bowl. From the amounts in this recipe I get 1 large and 1 medium.

Slice
3 eggplants
finely, lengthwise.
Dip in
milk,
then in
flour,
and fry in
olive oil
until golden.
In a pot heat some
olive oil
and add
1 eggplant chopped and cubed,
2 cloves garlic chopped,
1 tin Italian tomatoes (800 ml / 28 fl oz),
1 tsp oregano,
1 tsp parsley chopped.
Cook 5-6 minutes.
Season with
salt and pepper.

In another pot:
Cook
pasta
al dente,
drain and mix with the tomato sauce.
Add:
2 handfuls parmesan freshly grated,
250 ml / 1 cup cream or **yoghurt.**
Line a Pyrex bowl with eggplant slices, leaving overhang, fill half way with pasta, then add a layer of
mozzarella cubed.
Cover with more pasta.
Fold the eggplant overhang to cover the top.
Cook in a preheated oven at 175°C/350°F in a bain marie for 30 minutes.
Unmold by tipping upside down onto a serving plate.

Garnish with fresh basil and chopped tomatoes.

Serve with Bruno's tomato sauce (see page 70) which you purée and add some cream.

Bruno's pasta

A few years ago we had an Italian house guest called Bruno. At the end of his stay he wisely asked me what I would like as a present as he could see the garden was full of flowers and I don't often eat chocolate. Without hesitation I asked him if he could make a *real* tomato sauce. We jumped into the car, beetled down to the supermarket, purchased the few ingredients and 45 minutes later sat down to this, accompanied by breadsticks, pecorino, salad and of course, wine.

In a large pot sauté in
olive oil:
2 cloves of garlic halved,
2 onions chopped.
When limp add
1 large tin (800 ml / 28 fl oz)
of Italian tomatoes drained.
Crush all with a potato masher.
Add:
½ chicken stock cube
and simmer until thick.
(About 40 minutes)
Add
basil leaves torn
at the end and stir.

options:

- Keep the sauce in a jar - choose a jar that it will fill i.e. so that there's no air between the sauce and the lid. Keep in the fridge.

- Use it as a base for pizza - as is or blended.

- Serve it as is with any shape of pasta.

- Put in a blender and add some cream/milk to make it finer and more liquid and serve it either: on pasta as salsa rosa, or as a coulis on for example 'Pasta and eggplant Timbalo' page 69.

- Slice potatoes, put them in a bowl and add some of this tomato recipe. Mix so all the slices have some sauce. Spread in a roasting dish. Bake at 190°C/375°F for 20 minutes. Lay a whole fish on top of the potatoes and bake for another 20 minutes or until done. Easy and wickedly good. This immediately transports you to the Mediterranean sea shore.

note:

- If you have children (even fussy eaters) always keep this handy and always make a double batch.

Spaghetti alla Checca (Keka)

The beauty of this sauce is that you don't have to go anywhere near the stove, except to boil the pasta, and you don't have to do it at the last minute so you can swan out looking fresh as a daisy and preen when you hear the delighted noises of your guests *(well that's really what it's all about isn't it?)*

    Put into a salad bowl or a large mixing bowl:
1 kg / 2 lbs fresh Italian plum tomatoes
    cut into chunks,
10 - 20 garlic cloves,
    each cut into three.
    Mash with a fork.
    Add:
1 tbs dried oregano,
basil leaves torn,
dried red pepper flakes optional,
salt,
    and a lot of
olive oil.
    Mix and marinate - stir when you remember.
    Cook
spaghetti.
    Drain and add to the sauce in the bowl and toss.

And you'll never look back. This is it for summer.

Aspen Pastini (Ajax Tavern)

At the bottom of the slope in Aspen there is a wonderful restaurant called the Ajax Tavern. As I was waiting for Hossein to join me *(he skis - I've never got the hang of walking in those boots)*, I had ample opportunity to study the other diners' orders - I find this a much better way of choosing than reading a menu. This pasta dish with sausage looked wonderful and comforting. I ordered it and went back every day and had it for lunch. Unfortunately it was the first time that I had ever been refused a recipe, but not to be set back by some twit's arrogance I put a large spoonful in a paper napkin, returned to the hotel, put on my glasses and analysed the situation. This is what I came up with. It's delicious and fast.

Slice some
Italian sausage hot, medium or mild
and sauté until brown and crisp.
Drain on paper.
In another pan sauté in
olive oil:
4 garlic cloves chopped,
2 tomatoes chopped,
1 onion chopped,
handful of rapini chopped,
(or escarole or chard or anything green).
When partly cooked add a
tin of white beans rinsed.
Mix gently and keep warm.

For every
250 g / 8 oz. of Pastini,
boil
600 ml / 2½ cups chicken stock.
Cook Pastini in boiling chicken stock as indicated on the packet.
DO NOT DRAIN when cooked.
Just tip the whole lot into the bean/sausage/vegetable mix.
When combined put into a warm serving bowl and sprinkle the sausage rounds on top.

Serve with crusty bread, olive oil and freshly grated parmesan.

tips:

- I have no idea what Pastini is! I use a very small bead - like pasta called Ancini de Pepe.

- If you have vegetarians for this just serve the sausage separately in a dish at the table.

Risotto 4 Fromaggi

When our friend Michael Vineberg married Anna de Benedictus, little did we know what awaited us in the culinary department. And that wasn't all. She's one of the nicest people I know and she's beautiful. Some people have it all. The first time we had dinner in their home this was the first course followed by stuffed roast veal and apple pie. You can't improve on it so don't waste time trying to re-invent the wheel. Just do it - it's divine.

Cut into small cubes:
125 g / 4 oz gorgonzola,
125 g / 4 oz mozzarella,
125 g / 4 oz fontina or asiago,
(At this point you're saying "I thought it was four cheeses" keep reading)
and put into
1 cup milk / 8 fl oz / 250 ml warmed.
Set aside.

Heat in a pot:
125 g / 4 oz butter,
1 tbs olive oil.
Add:
450 g / 1 lb arborio rice
and sauté for 4 minutes.
Heat in another pot
900 ml / 3½ cups chicken broth cubes, tinned or fresh.
Add hot broth to rice, ladle by ladle until rice has absorbed it all.
Add few strands of
saffron crumbled
and melted in ladle full of broth.
Add milk with cheeses and keep stirring until fully amalgamated.
Add:
125 g / 4 oz Parmesan freshly grated
(there's your 4th cheese) and mix.
Serve.

tip:

- **Remember: Risotto waits for no-one.**

option:

- **You don't have to use the saffron.**
I do just to add some colour.

Universally loved and seldom made at home. I think there's this myth about having to have a wood burning stove with hot bricks and a long handled paddle and get covered in flour and go red from heat and end up looking very unattractive. Well it isn't so. Pizzas are easy, fun, healthy and creative. I make the dough, divide it into portions, put out about ten different toppings and let everyone get on with it! I used to think this was fun for kids, but I've come to the conclusion that adults like to do it even more so. Just remember that pizzas should be paper thin - *'just like a newspaper'* they say in Rome. Use Bruno's Pasta sauce (page 70) as a base and then put out bowls of: salami, ham, sliced tomatoes, sliced onions, mozarella, mushrooms, artichokes, olives, capers, and anything else you can think of. However if it's you who is doing them for your guests to have with drinks or as an amusing first course or as lunch with a salad then I suggest these toppings *(see right)*.

Pizzas

Dough:

Into a bowl put:
375 ml / 1½ cups warm water,
15 g / ½ oz of sugar,
30 g / 1 oz of dried yeast.
Leave to melt and bubble.
Add:
300 g / 10 oz flour,
1 tsp salt,
1 tsp olive oil.
Mix all together, gradually adding another
300 g / 10 oz flour.
Knead for 15-20 minutes, this actually is very therapeutic!
Put into an oiled bowl, cover and let rise in a draught-free place.
When risen, knead and cut into desired quantities.
Roll very thin, put onto a floured pizza pan,
brush with olive oil and spread with one of the following toppings: *(see right)*.

Preheat oven 200°C/400°F.

Toppings:

Spread dough with
onion *thinly sliced.*
Cook in the oven for 15 minutes.
Take out and spread with:
smoked salmon slices,
sour cream,
chopped chives.

or:

Sprinkle dough with
75 g grated fontina,
75 g grated mozzarella.
Cook in the oven until melted.
In a bowl toss some
arugola (roquette)
with a
balsamic vinaigrette
and spread over the cooked pizza.

or:

Sprinkle with
shaved parmesan.
Spread dough with
onion *thinly sliced,*
slices of ham or prosciutto,
slices of goat cheese,
black olives,
dried oregano,
olive oil.
Cook until the edges are crisp and the cheese is melted.

salads

Tomato, Basil and Crunchy Bacon	81
Corn Chaat	81
Crunchy Fennel and Parmesan	83
Apple, Endive and Stilton	84
Fattoush	85
Spinach	87

to die for!

Tomato, Basil and Crunchy Bacon Salad

Oh this is so good!

Slice in half about a
handful of cherry tomatoes
per person,
and add some
fresh basil torn.
In a small bowl mix:
balsamic vinegar,
olive oil.
Tip the dressing over the tomatoes and let sit.
Fry up some
cubes of bacon/lardons
until crisp and most of the oil has been rendered.
Drain on kitchen paper and put aside.
Just before serving tip the bacon bits over the salad -
DO NOT STIR.

Serve immediately - you see, if you stir you get soggy bacon and we wouldn't want that would we?

Corn Chaat

I have never met anyone who didn't like this recipe. It's fast, healthy and very refreshing.

In a serving bowl add:
1 tin corn niblets *(340 ml / 12 fl oz)*
drained,
1 cucumber peeled, seeded and diced,
1 medium red onion diced,
1 large tomato seeded and diced.
In a small bowl combine:
2 tbs lemon juice,
1 tsp fresh ginger grated,
1 tbs fresh cilantro leaves / coriander,
salt,
dash of cayenne pepper.

Pour over the salad, toss and refrigerate until time to serve.

Crunchy Fennel Salad with Parmesan

I'm always amazed at how many people think they don't like fennel. I'm doubly amazed when I serve them this or baked fennel and they want a second helping. Quite frankly you can never make enough of this.

Cut off the feathery leaves, stalks and root of some
fennel bulbs.
When cleaned up slice very thinly vertically *(I use a mandolin)*.
Lay half the fennel slices in a serving dish.
Sprinkle with
salt
and cover with a layer of
parmesan *shaved*
and then a layer of
parsley *coarsly chopped.*
Repeat fennel, salt, parmesan, parsley.
Sprinkle with
juice of 1 lemon
and
olive oil,
quite a lot!
Garnish with
lemon segments *quartered.*

note:

- Shave the parmesan with a vegetable peeler. If you are hung up on quantities this recipe should drive you nuts!

Apple, Endive and Stilton Salad

Vinaigrette:

In a bowl whisk together:
2 tbs white wine vinegar,
1 tbs red wine vinegar,
½ tsp dijon mustard,
½ tsp sugar,
2 tbs olive oil,
1 shallot minced,
salt and pepper.

Salad:

In a small pot melt
2 tbs butter.
Add:
125 g / 4 oz walnuts coarsely chopped,
½ tsp sugar.
Cook until crisp - watch carefully please.
Cut
endives
into julienne strips.
Cut
2 Granny Smith apples unpeeled
into fine slices.

Assembly:

In a salad bowl combine:
endives,
apples,
walnuts,
60 g / 2 oz Stilton crumbled
and the
vinaigrette.

Toss gently - to die for!

Fattoush

I love this salad.

Preheat oven 190°C/375°F.

With scissors snip
2 pita breads
into small rectangles (½" x ¾")
and place on a baking sheet.
Put in the oven tossing constantly until lightly toasted and crisp.
Reserve.

In a bowl mix:
1 cucumber peeled, seeded and chopped,
3 tomatoes seeded and chopped,
6 scallions chopped,
1 green pepper seeded and chopped,
handful of parsley chopped,
handful of mint chopped,
handful of fresh cilantro / coriander chopped,
and tender young leaves from the
centre of a Romaine lettuce chopped.

In a small bowl mix:
2 cloves garlic chopped,
juice of 1 lemon,
olive oil to taste,

and pour over the salad.

Toss all together, sprinkle with sumac and add the toasted pita chips just before serving to avoid them becoming limp and soggy. And again we wouldn't want that would we?

tip:

- Get Sumac at any middle eastern grocery shop. It's delicious and does make a difference.

Spinach Salad

This and the recipe for *Roast Milkfed Lamb* are undeniably the simplest recipes in this book.

Sauté in some
butter
and
sugar
some
walnuts *chopped.*
Cool.
Combine:
spinach leaves *washed and dried,*
(the younger the more tender),
raisins
or
sour cherries
or
pomegranate seeds,
scallions *thinly sliced,*
1 green apple *unpeeled and thinly sliced,*
Feta cheese *crumbled,*
and the sautéed walnuts.

Dressing Ratio:

2 tsp apple cider vinegar.
2 tbs olive oil.

Toss all together with gay abandon.

meat & poultry

Agnello al Forno	90
Milk-fed Lamb *(Emiliano)*	92
Rack of Lamb	94
Lamb Shanks with Rosemary	95
Chicken with 30 Cloves of Garlic	96
Duck Breasts and Honeyed Turnips	98
Coq au Vin *(Olivier)*	100
Saltimbocca a la Romana	102
Pot au Feu	104
One Pot Beef and Capers	105
Tagliata	106
Beef Stroganoff	108
Entrecôte Vigneron	108
Sauce Roquefort	109
Choucroute Garnie	110
Oxtail Braised in Wine	111

to die for!

Agnello Al Forno

I love lamb and this is just about as good as it gets, thanks to Diana.

Preheat oven 230°C/450°F.

Rub
lamb leg
with
lemon.
Stick it with many
garlic slivers *finely sliced*
and
rosemary branches
(i.e. it should look like a hedgehog).
Put in a roasting pan and sprinkle with
white wine
and
salt and pepper.
NO oil or butter.
Lower oven to 190°C/375°F and roast for 2 hours.

note:

- **Only the French eat undercooked meat. Elsewhere in Europe they like it cooked and caramelised.**

- **Don't puncture the lamb vertically to stick in the garlic and rosemary, do it horizontally to avoid breaking the tendons and blood vessels. You get a moister roast this way.**

Milk-fed Lamb *(Emiliano)*

Cordero Lechal

This is the simplest recipe in the book. The key is that the lamb must be milk fed lamb. It is a traditional Spanish dish along with milk fed baby pig - Cochinillo. My friend Emiliano is a sheep trader - who better to give me the recipe?

Preheat oven 150°C/300°F.

Put ¼" water in a baking pan.
Place on top
a lamb leg or **a half of a lamb.**
(They are very small).
Sprinkle with
salt.
Cook for 2 - 3 hrs.
It falls off the bone and you will always remember the taste.

Serve only with
romaine lettuce
dressed with
olive oil and vinegar.

Roast Rack of Lamb

In 1990 our house burned down - everything except the outside walls. After much soul searching we decided to rebuild but that doesn't happen immediately because there are architects, planning committee approval, contractors, etc, etc to see before anything physical takes place. My good friend Martha Fruchet could see clearly that I was a little at sea and needed an immediate project so she asked me to give a cooking course for four of her friends at her house in the country. I thought she was mad but I agreed and planned a menu and took all my equipment. The menu was - *Tartare de Saumon, Rack of Lamb, Potato Gratin and Crème Brulée.*
I had never given a class on anything in my life. The next sequence in the story is that five weeks later there were 22 people in the class. I had found an outlet for my passion and will always be eternally grateful to Martha.

Preheat oven 200°C/400°F.

Roast some
racks of lamb trimmed and frenched
for 15 minutes - this can be done a few hours before serving.
(I allow 3 chops per person.)
When cool spread with a layer of
dijon mustard.
Dip into a mixture of:
breadcrumbs,
parsley chopped,
thyme chopped,
rosemary chopped.
Place in the oven for 25-30 minutes - each chop will be pink.
If you don t believe me take out 1 rack and cut in half.
Judge for yourself if you would like it cooked more.

Lamb Shanks with Rosemary

Sauce for roast rack of lamb:

Preheat oven 230°C/450°F.

Roast
some lamb bones
(that your nice butcher has given you)
for 15 minutes.
Add a mirepoix of :
3 carrots diced,
2 leeks chopped.
Continue roasting for 5 minutes.
Tip everything carefully into a pot on top of the stove.
Add:
a shot of vermouth.
Sizzle and add:
water or chicken stock,
bay leaf,
rosemary,
thyme,
2 squirts of tomato paste
(or 2 fresh tomatoes chopped).
Boil, simmer, strain, refridgerate and skim off any fat that has solidified. Reduce over high heat and believe it or not
add some
mint finely chopped,
JUST BEFORE SERVING.

I've always been a fan of the shank. I love bones. Fortunately they seem to be more popular these days so they are more available. I can remember scouring the city for them before.

Preheat oven 175°C/350°F.

Allow
1 lamb shank
per person.
In a casserole sauté the shanks
in
olive oil
until lightly browned.
Add:
16 cloves of garlic unpeeled,
2 glasses white wine,
4 rosemary sprigs,
salt and pepper.
Put the lid on the casserole and cook in the oven for 1½ - 2 hrs. When ready take out meat and keep warm.
Skim the fat off the juices and pour over the meat.

Utterly delicious with mashed potato and / or white beans.

Chicken with 30 Cloves of Garlic

You'll notice that this is very similar to the lamb shanks recipe. I've included them both because they are absolutely delicious yet different and so quick to prepare. They are both staple meals in our house.

Preheat oven 200°C/400°F.

Pat dry
a chicken.
Melt some
butter and olive oil
in a casserole until pretty hot and then brown the bird all over.
Remove.
To the casserole add:
30 garlic cloves unpeeled,
(or as many as you've got)
6 small sprigs rosemary.
Toss and replace the chicken.
Add:
300 ml / 10 oz white wine.
Sprinkle with
1 tbs chopped rosemary
and gently bring to a simmer.
Cover and bake in the oven 1½ hrs.
Remove the lid and continue 10 minutes.
Remove and rest 10 minutes.
Carve and serve with garlic cloves and juices.

Brilliant with mashed potatoes.

tip:

- As in the lamb shanks recipe (page 95), it is better to skim the fat off the juices.

Duck Breasts and Honeyed Turnips

Magret de Canard et Navets au Miel à la manière de Dominique

Dominique Bourgeois is a friend of mine in Paris and one of the best cooks I know and at whose table I have enjoyed many a wonderful, uncomplicated meal. She is the essence of 'chic' and totally understated. I first tasted this combination at her home and it quickly became a favourite. We always have this on Christmas eve, preceded by oysters and followed by crème caramel - that way we can still cope with Christmas day! I've put them on the same page because they go together so brilliantly - just like Harry and Sophie, my twin bassets.

Duck:

Spread a frying pan with
coarse salt
and heat until very hot.
Put the
duck breast(s)
skin side down on the salt.
Cook for 6 - 8 minutes until brown.
Turn and continue to cook for 6 - 8 minutes.
When done put them in a warm oven and leave them to settle.
Slice them, not too thinly, and spoon the juices over the top.

Honeyed Turnips:

Peel, cut into chunks and boil in salted water
turnips, *the white ones with purple bottoms.*
Drain.
Melt
2 tbs butter
and sauté
4 french shallots *minced*
until golden.
Add:
3 tbs honey
and boil 3 - 4 minutes.
Add:
2 tbs white vinegar
and boil 3 - 4 minutes.
Sauté the boiled turnips in another pan in
butter
until they are golden. Mix the turnips and the sauce gently together.

note:

- These can be made ahead of time and reheated before serving.

Coq au Vin *(Olivier)*

This is a very important recipe as it solves a little confusion. You see if you do this with beef instead of a coq then you get Boeuf Bourguignon and if you do it with a coq and Riesling *(white wine)* you get Coq au Riesling. Please remember that a coq is not a chicken, try to get the real thing. If you can't, then get a capon.

note:

- This is always better the day after you make it and it also allows you to de-grease it when you remove it from the fridge.

- This freezes very well - however, freeze the mushrooms and onions separately and add them 20 minutes before serving. (Otherwise they disintegrate)

In a heavy casserole melt
2 tbs butter.
Cook
125 g / 4 oz fresh lardon cut in strips,
12 white button onions peeled.
In a separate pan melt
2 tbs butter
and sauté
250 g / 8 oz mushrooms cleaned and quartered.
When onions and lardons are browned strain and put aside.
Into the same fat put
1 coq cut into pieces
and sauté until golden.
Sprinkle with
30 g / 1 oz flour
and brown some more.
Add:
2 garlic cloves chopped,
1 bottle Bourgogne red wine.
Boil, add the mushrooms, onions, lardons and
1 bouquet garni,
3 tbs cognac,
salt and pepper.
Flambée and simmer for 2½ hrs or until tender.
Remove coq, onions, mushrooms, lardons and keep hot.
Strain sauce,
season and keep over low heat.
Arrange coq and vegetables on a plate, cover with sauce and sprinkle with
parsley chopped.

Serve with triangular croutons and mashed potatoes.

Saltimbocca alla Romana

I haven't met anyone who didn't like this.
It's easy, fresh and delicious. Super casual dinner fare.

Pound some
veal scallopine
between 2 layers of
wax paper
and cut each piece in half.
Fold a piece of
prosciutto
to the size of the veal slice.
Add:
1 sage leaf
and attach all three with a toothpick.
Dredge in some
flour
lightly and sauté in
olive oil.
When done, keep warm and swill the juices with some
white wine.
Pour over the veal.

note:

- **VERY IMPORTANT** - tell your guests about the toothpick.

- Very good with sautéed red peppers and green salad.

Pot Au Feu

My absolute favourite.

In a large pot place any two or all of the following:
500g / 1 lb loin of pork,
500g / 1 lb blade of beef,
500g / 1 lb leg of lamb,
315g / 10 oz streaky bacon (no rind),
1 shin of veal,
1 chicken.

Cover with cold water and bring to the boil for 1 minute. Take out the meats and chicken and rinse under cold water. Throw the stock away, clean the pot. *(If you miss this step you get murky broth).*
Replace the meats and chicken and fill with cold water, enough to cover by ¼".
Add:
a bouquet garni,
salt
and bring to a gentle boil. Lower heat and skim constantly. Cover but leave a small gap for steam and simmer gently. After 1 hour remove the chicken and keep warm on a plate covered with foil.
After 2 hours add
6 large carrots peeled and cut into chunks.
After a further 15 minutes add:
2 turnips cut in 4,
3 leeks cut in 2 and tied,
24 baby white onions peeled,
2 parsnips cut into chunks.
Continue simmering gently until the vegetables are done. Taste broth, correct seasoning and put the chicken back in to warm up.

Serve with rock salt, mustards and pickles.

tips:

- It can also be served with cabbage, but cook it separately.

- Traditionally the broth is served first and the meats and vegetables follow on a large platter.

options:

- It's also wonderful done with only veal shanks and vegetables, then it becomes 'Jarret de Veau à l'ancienne.'

- If you do this with only chicken it becomes 'Poule au Pot.' Just cut down on the cooking time.

One Pot Beef and Capers

Soak in milk
4 anchovies.
Soak in water
2 tbs drained capers.
Whilst they are doing their thing *(soaking)* combine in a large bowl:
796 ml / 28 oz tin of Italian tomatoes *drained,*
2 onions *finely sliced,*
6 small cornichons (gherkins) *finely sliced,*
salt.
Mix gently making sure to break up the tomatoes and add the drained capers and anchovies.
Cut
1 kg / 2 lbs of beef
into 1½" slices. *(I like flank steak).*
In a pot simmer
1 bottle of white wine
for 10 minutes.
In a heavy casserole spread:
⅓ of the tomato mixture,
1 bay leaf,
sprig of thyme,
2-3 slices of meat,
salt and pepper.
Repeat another two times but without the bay leaf and the thyme. Gently pour the wine over everything and bring it to a simmer. Cover and simmer 2 hours, checking from time to time and stirring gently.
DO NOT BOIL.
When done remove bay leaf and thyme, cool, refrigerate, degrease, reheat and serve.

notes:

- **You can make this up to three days in advance.**

- **Always wonderful with mashed potatoes.**

- **I've started dividing it into iron casseroles that hold enough for 2 people. I then put it on a protective mat on the table between each 2 guests and they go to it. It keeps their second portions warm, doesn't mean you have to serve, and basically means everyone can get on with it at their own speed.**

Tagliata

When I went on a cooking course in Italy we had a day trip to Perugia. I asked one of the girls working in the school where I should go for lunch. She not only told me where but she also told me what to eat. I am eternally grateful to her and so are many of my friends and students.
If you've never had it, try it - it's divine.

You need some
sirloin steak
cut into thin, thin slices *(just a little thicker than carpaccio)*.
Flash fry in HOT
olive oil
and keep warm.
Serve on a bed of
arugola (roquette)
and sprinkle with:
salt and pepper,
parmesan shaved,
olive oil,
lemon juice.

Serve immediately - and I mean immediately.

Beef Stroganoff

I'd never been impressed one way or another with beef Stroganoff until I had it made by Vari Dehesh, a Persian friend and a wonderful cook. Then I became addicted - it's the cumin you see!

Sauté
1 onion chopped.
Add:
beef fillet sliced and cut into strips.
In another pan, sauté some
mushrooms sliced
and sprinkle with
flour.
Add:
a chicken cube crumbled
to the onion and meat.
Add a sprinkling of
powdered garlic - yes, powdered garlic,
½ tsp ground cumin,
2-3 tsp tomato paste,
salt and pepper.
Add the mushrooms and
a little water.
Before serving, add a little
cream
and stir until warm.
Sprinkle with an abundance of
matchstick potatoes.
(In the US you can buy these in a tin and just heat them up - amazing)!

This is wonderful served with a simple Boston lettuce salad.

Entrecôte Vigneron

Every so often I must have a steak. It must be my need to chew but I can't rest until I eat one. This recipe more than satisfies me and is an ideal dinner party dish accompanied by potato gratin.

Finely chop
3 french shallots,
1 medium onion,
2 anchovies.
Reserve.
Melt
50 g / 1½ oz butter
in a pan until very hot.
Season
1 thick rib steak boneless (875 g/1¾ lbs),
with
salt and pepper.
Cook steak for 8 minutes per side, put on a warm plate and keep warm in the oven.
Stir the onion mixture into the used pan and cook for 5 minutes constantly stirring.
Add:
125 ml / ½ cup of red wine.
Boil 1-2 minutes until thickened slightly.
Strain.
Cut steak into large pieces and add the juices to the sauce.
Pour the sauce over the top.

note:
- 1 rib = 3 persons.

Sauce Roquefort

A few years ago we stayed for a month in a hotel in Uzès. There was a young couple working there who were charming and even walked my dogs at night if we were out. They said that at the end of the season they were going to spend 6 months going around the world and thought that as Montreal was French speaking, that would be a good place to start.
We agreed with them and told them to stay with us as we had ample room. So they did - for 5 months! He was a trained cook and he taught me this.
It's easy and to die for.

    Put in a small pot of water
½ Knorr beef cube.
    Boil and reduce - this gives you your stock.
    Cook some
steaks *(obviously 1 per person)*
    and keep warm.
    Add the beef stock to the steak pan and add
a touch of cream.
    Reduce.
    Add some
roquefort *crumbled,*
    stirring constantly until melted.
    Add:
2 nuggets of butter
    and
the juices
    which have by now come out of the steaks.
    Simmer and pour the whole thing on top of the steaks.

OHHHHH!

Choucroute Garnie

For years I would revel in this dish throughout restaurants in France, always thinking what a shame that no-one ever did it at home. Back in Canada we went to our friends Margot and Jerry Pagé's for dinner and she did the most wonderful choucroute I've ever tasted. So the next day I got out all my books, got a rough idea of what the method was and to my amazement discovered there was barely any cooking to be done. It is essentially warming and assembling the ingredients. No wonder most French bistros and brasseries have it on the menu.

Preheat oven 175°C/350°F.

In a pestle crush a few
juniper berries
and reserve.
Make a spice bag of cheese cloth and put in:
6 cloves,
15 juniper berries,
4 bay leaves,
4 garlic cloves.
Open
3 tins of choucroute 'Kuhne'.
Rinse one in cold water and then mix this with the other two.
Sauté in a large pan
lardons diced.
When melted add
2 onions chopped.
Add:
choucroute,
2 cups Riesling white wine,
1 cup water,
salt and pepper,
the spice bag and the reserved junipers.
Stir and heat through in the oven.
Put
meat
(list of choices opposite) in to heat through, (I put mine on top of the choucroute), and cover with foil.

Place the meats and sausages in the middle of the plate and spread the cabbage around the edge.

Serve with mustards and mashed potatoes.

meats for choucroute:

sliced ham,
smoked bacon in one piece,
kasle (cooked pork chops),

frankfurters or strasbourg sausage,
smoked sausages or
colmar sausages,
bratwurst.
Heat all sausage in simmering water.

note:

● The meats must be heated through.

Oxtail Braised in Wine

Oxtail has been totally underrated for years. I'm so pleased to see at last that it's gaining in popularity.

Preheat oven 175°C/350°F.

In a heavy casserole sauté in a mixture of
olive oil and butter:
handful of parsley chopped,
2 garlic cloves finely chopped,
2 onions chopped,
4 carrots chopped.

Cook for 10 minutes, stirring often.
Raise the heat and add:
1.25 kg / 2½ lb ox tail
and
250 g / 8 oz thick bacon/lardon, sliced and diced.
Sauté until all is brown.
Add:
375 ml / 1½ cups dry white wine
and boil for 3 minutes.
Add:
a small tin of Italian tomatoes drained and chopped,
250 ml / 1 cup of water,
salt and pepper.
When simmering cover and put in the oven for 2 hours, turning the meat every ½ hour.
Before serving take off as much fat as possible.

Serve with real mashed potatoes.

notes:

- **Ideally this dish should be cooked for 1½ hours, a day beforehand, skimmed of fat, and gently reheated for 1 hour.**

- **This freezes with fabulous results.**

- **In Spain the meat is removed and kept warm and the sauce and vegetables put in a blender and served as a puréed sauce.**

fish

Roast Salmon	114
Sauce for Grilled Fish 1	114
Sauce for Grilled Fish 2	114
Fish in Salt	116
La Lotte à la Manière de Dominique	117
Gulai Ikan (Malaysian Fish Curry)	118
My Simple Fish Soup	120

to die for!

Roast Salmon

Trust me on this one.

Preheat oven 200°C/400°F.

Spread a non-stick baking tray with a layer of **coarse salt.**
Lay
a whole fillet of salmon (skin on)
or cut the fillet into serving pieces
and lay on top of the salt.
Bake for about 12 minutes.
That's it.

note:

- If you want it to be really golden on top paint it with a thin layer of mayonnaise before cooking.

(you never heard me say that).

Sauce for Grilled Fish

Chop finely by HAND:
handful of mint leaves washed and dried,
handful of parsley leaves washed and dried,
1-2 large garlic cloves.
Put in a sauce boat and slowly add:
olive oil,
pepper,
juice of ½ lemon,
2 drops red wine vinegar.

note:

- Very good with swordfish steaks and halibut.

Another Sauce for Grilled Fish

Put into a food processor or blender:
1 small red pepper,
½ cup white onions,
1 clove garlic,
½ cup fresh coriander,
½ cup olive oil,
2 tbs red wine vinegar,
salt and pepper.

Aye! Aye! Aye! Caramba!

Fish in Salt

This is a simple, healthy and impressive way to serve fish. I've only ever seen it on the Spanish coast but I serve it a lot at home to the delight of my guests. I serve it only with a romaine lettuce salad and sliced tomatoes. Coarse salt is cheap so don't be stingy, make sure the whole fish is firmly ensconced.

Preheat oven 175°C/350°F.

In an oven dish large enough for the whole fish, pour a fairly thick layer of **course salt** *(buy a big bag)*.
Lay the
fish
on top *(head and tail intact but guts cleaned)* and cover with more salt.
Pat firmly into place.
At this point you should be looking at a dish completely covered in salt with a hump in it.
Put into the oven and bake 45-55 minutes.

To serve tap the crust and lift it off the fish.

Take off the skin and serve with:
**lemon halves,
good olive oil,
salt and pepper**
or
garlic infused warm olive oil.

notes:

- I give everyone a bit of the salt crust.

- **This is a fantastic dish for anyone with cholesterol problems.**

- **I have a preference to do this recipe with striped bass, but I am sure red snapper or dorade would be just as good.**

La Lotte à la Manière de Dominique

This is the same Dominique as she of the Magret and honeyed turnips. She told me something that I've never forgotten - treat the monkfish the same as you would a leg of lamb. Psychologically this helps as this has to be one of the ugliest fish created, but the good thing is it has no bones, just a central cartilage so it's easy to serve.

Preheat oven 200°C/400°F.

Wipe dry

a large lotte (monkfish)

and stick it with

garlic slices,

as you would a leg of lamb.

Mix 2-3 tbs coriander seeds crushed,

with some

olive oil

and pour over the fish.
Let sit for 2 hours.
Put it in the oven and after 15 minutes add

salt and pepper

and

1-2 tbs Pernod.

Put back in the oven until done (20-30 minutes).
Remove the fish and keep warm.
Mix juice with

cream,

just enough to change the colour of the sauce,
and add

dill chopped

and

fresh coriander / cilantro chopped.

Heat gently and spoon some over the fish.
Serve the rest in a warmed sauceboat.

Good with braised endives.

Malaysian Fish Curry
Gulai Ikan

This is divine - especially if you're prone to curry attacks. It's so simple to make and smooth to taste. It's not Thai and it's not Indian. It's Malaysian - gentle and fine, just like the people. You've probably guessed by now that I like anything and everything about Malaysia - I used to live there when it was still Malaya. *I loved it.*

Put in a food processor:
2 medium onions chopped,
2 cloves garlic chopped,
2 tsp fresh ginger peeled and chopped,
1 tsp sambal oelek*.
  Put the mixture into a pot and rinse the bowl with
1 cup thin coconut milk.
  Add:
1 tbs ground coriander,
1 tsp ground cumin,
½ tsp ground fennel,
½ tsp ground turmeric,
2 strips lemon rind,
6 curry leaves.
  Boil, reduce heat, simmer 8 minutes
  and add
500 g / 1lb white fish (halibut, turbot),
  cut into bite sized pieces.

or:
2 large shelled shrimps per person.
  Also add:
2 tbs lemon juice,
1 tsp salt.
  Simmer 5 minutes
  and add
½ cup thick coconut milk.
  Stir until it simmers and the fish is cooked through, (but not falling apart).

Served with boiled rice - basmati of course.

tips:

● Don't shake the tin of coconut milk. The top part is thick and should be saved for the last step and the bottom is thin and is used at the beginning.

● Unexpected guests? Hard boil some eggs, shell, cut in half lengthwise, add them to the pot. *DIVINE!*

* Sambal oelek is readily available at Oriental food shops.

My Simple Fish Soup

In Canada lobsters are plentiful and in season they are inexpensive. As they are also easy to cook anyone can put a meal together of *'fresh asparagus with oil and lemon; boiled lobster with lemon butter; strawberries and cream'*. In fact I can't keep track of how many times I've had that menu *(the other standbys are poached cold or hot whole salmon or roast whole fillet of beef)*. When I serve lobster I make sure I have 2 bowls for the shells - 1 for the shells people have been gnawing on which go straight into the bin and the other for those which haven't. Those that haven't get frozen in plastic bags and when I have to make a bisque I've already got my shells. When I do this soup I like to use halibut because it's solid and cubes well.

Chop
2 large onions *(or 01 onion and 2 leeks).*
Sauté in
olive oil,
and when opaque add
lobster shells *crushed.*
Keep sautéeing for 5 minutes and add:
4 tomatoes *chopped,*
or
4 squirts of tomato paste.
thyme,
bay leaf,
parsley sprigs,
1 cup of white wine.
Cook and stir over high heat.
Add:
water
to cover,
a fish bouillon cube,
salt and pepper.

Simmer on low heat.
Go about your business until you remember something is cooking.
Strain liquid into a clean pot and throw away the rest.
Peel and cube
3 potatoes
and cook in a separate pot with water until soft but not mushy.
In a small bowl crush
1 tsp of saffron
and add some of the fish stock.
Mix and tip into the pot of stock.
Add:
shrimps,
scallops,
fish chunks,
potatoes.
Cook gently until done.

You'll never look back!

vegetables

Potato and Ham Pie / Flan / Soufflé	124
Potato, Mushroom and Cheese Casserole	126
Potato Gratin	127
Potato Gratin *(Nice and Crunchy)*	127
Roast Tomatoes	128
Tortino di Pomodoro *(An alternative to roast tomatoes)*	128
Braised Escarole	130
Braised Fennel	131
Courgette Flan	132
Melanzane alla Parmigiana	134
Zucchine al Pinoli	136

to die for!

Potato and Ham Pie/Flan/Soufflé

Basically men like meat and potatoes. They may not say it, they may even deny it, but the truth is that they do. So give it to them when you want them to be happy. Works like a charm. This is a version of one of Diana's recipes.

Preheat oven 200°C/400°F.

Rule of thumb:
1 potato per person plus 1 for the pot.
This recipe is based on 8 potatoes.
Boil the
potatoes *with their skins on.*
Peel and put through a ricer.
Add:
salt and pepper,
45 g / 1½ oz butter,
2 eggs,
150 mls / ⅔ cup heavy cream,
375 g / ¾ lb fresh mozzarella *cubed,*
250 g / ½ lb ham *cut in thick slices, stacked and cubed,*
8 tbs parmesan *freshly grated,*
some nutmeg *freshly grated.*

Butter
a soufflé dish and sprinkle with
breadcrumbs.
Tip potato mix in, dot with butter
and sprinkle breadcrumbs over top.
Bake for 45-50 minutes.
When done, turn off the oven and leave
until ready to serve.

Potato, Mushroom & Cheese Casserole

This is just so good - try it and you'll see what I mean.

Preheat oven 190°C/375°F.

Chop coarsely
12 mushrooms,
and sauté in
butter.
Peel and slice thinly
1 kg / 2 lb potatoes.
In a buttered baking dish layer:
potatoes,
mushrooms,
mozzarella sliced,
strong cheddar sliced.
Repeat as often as you have ingredients always ending in potatoes.
Mix in a bowl:
100 ml / ⅓ cup heavy cream,
60 ml / ¼ cup white wine,
60 ml / ¼ cup chicken stock.
Pour over the potatoes.
Bake 1 hour or until golden,
whichever comes first.

Potato Gratin

Preheat oven 175°C/350°F.

Finely slice:
1 medium onion
 and
125 g / 4 oz of leek
 and sauté for about 5 mins in
olive oil.
 Add:
500 g / 1 lb raw potatoes sliced,
150 mls / ²⁄₃ cup chicken broth,
150 mls / ²⁄₃ cup white wine
 and cook for a further 15 minutes. Transfer to a baking dish and put in the oven until golden.

If you don't think this is to die for, then you have no taste!

Potato Gratin
(Nice and Crunchy)

Preheat oven 200°C/400°F.

Put in a bowl, peeled and thinly sliced
potatoes.
 Add:
gruyère grated,
olive oil a little,
fresh thyme leaves,
salt and pepper,
chicken stock.
 Mix with hands and lay in an overlapping circular pattern, layer upon layer in non-stick cake tins.
 Bake for 45 minutes or until brown and crunchy on the outside and soft inside.

note:

- It stands to reason that if you like cheese you add quite a bit, and if you don't like it you put in less - same goes for the thyme.

Roast Tomatoes (Orvieto)

Fresh Italian plum tomatoes don't really have much flavour unless you marinate them as in Pasta alla Checka or unless you roast them like this. If after the 40 minutes cooking you think they could be even drier - pop them back in. The less moisture the more flavour. Ideal with roast lamb.

Preheat oven 200°C/400°F.

Cut in half lengthwise
fresh Italian plum tomatoes.
Lay on a non-stick baking tray.
Sprinkle with:
garlic chopped,
oregano dried,
salt and pepper,
olive oil.
Bake for 40 minutes, place on serving dish and sprinkle with
fresh basil sliced finely.

Tortino di Pomodoro

An alternative to the roast tomatoes.

Preheat oven 180°C/350°F.

Wash and dry
perfect tomatoes.
Cut in half horizontally and de-seed them with your thumb.
In a bowl mix:
6 tbs bread crumbs,
4 tbs parmesan freshly grated,
4 tbs Italian parsley chopped,
2 tsp capers,
2 cloves garlic chopped,
salt and pepper.
Moisten with a little water and
olive oil.
Line up the tomatoes on a non-stick baking tray and top them with the mixture, pushing into holes with your index finger.
Roast 40 minutes - 1 hr.

• **Roast Tomato (Orvieto)**

Braised Escarole

This was originally a pie that Diana Folonari taught in her classes. I don't like cooked spinach so I'm always on the look out for an alternative green. I love cooked escarole and rapini so I often cook them this way and serve them as a vegetable and forget about the pastry.

In a large frying pan sauté in
olive oil:
½ **jar black olives** pitted by you,
½ **jar green olives** pitted by you,
5 to 6 cloves garlic (each cut in 3),
½ **tin anchovies** minced,
½ **cup capers.**
Sauté until anchovies melt and add
1½ **heads of escarole** washed and spun.
Cook on medium heat until limp.
Add some
red pepper flakes (optional).
Increase heat to evaporate juice.
Cool and dress with
olive oil.
Or treat as you would Margherita's Onion Pie.
(Page 37)

Braised Fennel

This recipe should be a killer for those of you who are still hung up on quantities - *LIVE DANGEROUSLY!*

Wash and trim and cut into segments
some fennel bulbs.

Heat
olive oil
and sauté for 1-2 minutes
some thin slices of garlic,
and
a little sugar.
Add fennel segments
and sauté until golden.
Add some
fresh orange juice or **chicken stock,**
water,
salt and pepper.
Cover and simmer until tender.

note:

- If you think this is too simple, tip it into a baking dish, top with grated parmesan, put it in the oven until brown and voilà - '*Gratin de Fenouil*'!

Courgette Flan

I once had 'flan aux champignons' at the Fontaine de Mars. Again I chose it because it looked so good on my neighbour's plate. I asked the very charming owner how to do it and she said eggs, cream and cêpes. So this is what I came up with. If doing it with mushrooms, I add some parsley. If doing it with tomatoes I sauté them over a high heat to get rid of their juice.

Preheat Oven 175°C/350°F.

Finely slice

1 onion,

and finely slice

3 courgettes

(or the equivalent volume of mushrooms or tomatoes).
Put both together in a frying pan with some

olive oil

and sauté gently with the lid on until limp *BUT NOT BROWN*.
Uncover and boil off some of the liquid.
Put into a food processor and spin until chopped up.
While spinning add:

3 eggs,
¼ cup of cream,
3 tbs of parmesan *freshly grated,*
salt and pepper.

Put into either a medium soufflé dish or small individual ones and cook in a bain-marie for 1 hour.
Obviously you cook them for less time if you use the individual ones.

note:

- Did you know that cêpes are the same as porcini?
Well now you do.

Melanzane alla Parmigiana

This is so simple and so good you'll wonder why on earth you didn't think of it before.

Preheat oven 200°C/400°F.

Peel and slice lengthwise
4 medium eggplants.
Pat dry and dredge in
flour.
Fry in very hot
olive oil
(if it's not hot enough the eggplant will suck it up like a sponge).

Layer a buttered dish with:
the fried eggplant slices,
tinned Italian tomatoes drained and chopped,
fresh basil leaves torn,
parmesan freshly grated.
Repeat as often as you have ingredients, always ending in cheese.
Bake 15 to 25 minutes.
Let settle before serving.

notes:

- **This can be made 2 to 3 days ahead.**

- **It's very good cold.**

Zucchine al Pinoli

My goodness this is popular. The key is not to cook them too much otherwise they go soggy - keep them crunchy.

Heat
2 tbs olive oil
until just smoking.
In a bowl toss:
courgettes *sliced on the diagonal,*
handful of pine nuts,
5 cloves of garlic *chopped.*
Sauté briefly until golden but still firm.
Put in a serving bowl and toss with
mint *finely chopped.*

Drop dead delicious!

desserts

Crème Caramel	140
Crème Brûlée	142
Fruit Soup	144
Fruit Soup 2	144
Pears in Marsala	146
Tarte Tatin	148
Sarah D'Arcy's Secret Tuile	150
Berries with Kirsch and Mint	152
Chilled Orange Slices	153
Nicole's Chocolate Truffle Cake	154

to die for!

Crème Caramel

This is so good.
In Spain almost every meal ends with this or with fresh fruit in a bowl of water.

Caramel:

In a small pot combine:
180 g / 6 oz sugar,
3 tbs of water.
Boil until golden.
Watch carefully, it changes colour suddenly.
Pour into the bottom of a mould and let cool until hardened.

Preheat oven 175°C/350°F.

Flan:

Scald
1.25 litres / 1 quart milk.
Put into a mixer:
5 whole eggs,
4 egg yolks,
½ tsp vanilla,
60 g / 2 oz sugar.
Gradually add the hot milk and strain everything into the mould.
Let rest 10 minutes.
Put the mould into a bain marie and cook for about 1 hour or until it is set.
Cool and chill for a minimum of 6 hrs.

Unmoulding:

Put the cold mould into a shallow dish of hot water for 1 minute to melt the caramel and slice around the edge.
Invert onto a serving dish with a rim to catch the caramel.

tips:

- I always make mine in a Charlotte mould - they're a little higher and narrower than the standard. Rather impressive (such a show off!).

- I use a thin wooden skewer to test for 'doneness'.

Crème Brûlée

Remember this is a cream, as in custard, not as in flan. I serve this with either berries or chilled oranges.

Preheat oven 175°C/350°F.

Scald
750 ml / 3 cups of heavy cream
in a double boiler over simmering water *(scalding is just before boiling)*.
Add:
6 tbs sugar.
Stir until melted.
In a food processor mix
6 egg yolks
and gradually add the hot, sweetened cream.
Stir in
1 tsp vanilla
and strain into a dish which you've already put in a bain marie.
Bake 35-40 minutes or until still a little wobbly but not too liquid.
Chill *(better if overnight)*.
Sprinkle every pore of the surface with
brown sugar *(cassonade)*
and broil.
WATCH CAREFULLY!

note:

- **I make mine in a quiche dish - very pretty.**

Fruit Soup

These two recipes are simplicity itself. Serve them with biscotti.

Make a sugar syrup by dissolving an amount of
sugar
in an equal amount of
water.
In a food processor, blend a defrosted packet of
raspberries.
Add:
some water / sugar syrup,
some
Cointreau or **Triple Sec** or **Grand Marnier**
or anything else you've got.
Add:
some sliced strawberries.
CHILL and add
mint leaves
to each bowl.

note:

- **Don't use all the water/sugar syrup, just enough to suit your taste. Keep the rest in the fridge.**

Another Fruit Soup

We first tasted this at Fouquet's at the Opera de la Bastille in Paris. This recipe was memorable. The performance was not! One out of two ain't bad!

Mix gently together in a serving bowl :
sliced strawberries,
orange segments,
green grapes peeled and sliced in half.
Add:
some white wine,
some water/sugar syrup
(see opposite).
Chill and add
mint leaves
before serving.

Pears in Marsala

If this takes you more than five minutes to prepare, you are doing something wrong. If anybody leaves anything other than the core on their plate you've definitely done something wrong.

Preheat oven 175°C/350°F.

Wash and stand
unpeeled pears *with stems intact,*
in a baking dish.
If they wobble cut the underside straight to give them balance.
Pour
250 ml / 1 cup dry marsala,
150 ml / ⅔ cup water
over the pears.
Sprinkle with
250 g / 8 oz sugar.
Add:
1 cinnamon stick.
Bake for 2 hours, basting every 20 minutes or when you remember.
Serve at room temperature with sifted icing sugar over the top
(if you want to impress).

Tarte Tatin

This is the recipe for an authentic Tarte Tatin - all others pale in comparison. It was given to me by Mme Yvette in the Vaucluse who is a feisty 80 something year old and an ex resistance runner. She is tall, large and definitely not someone to stand any nonsense but she's the salt of the earth, and has a great sense of humour. Amongst my students this is the number one favourite and Crème Brulée is the runner up. For this divine dessert you will need a metal pan that will go in the oven and on top of the oven. Once you've solved this problem there's nothing stopping you.

Pastry: *(enough for 2 tarts)*

Mix in a bowl:
250 g / 8 oz flour,
50 g / 1 ½ oz sugar,
pinch of salt.

Add:
1 egg,
1 tbs sunflower oil,
125 g / 4 oz cold butter *cut into little pieces.*

Sand with fingertips until you can make two firm balls and the bowl is clean.
Wrap in plastic and put in the fridge.

note:

- **The second ball of pastry can be frozen for eternity or kept in the fridge for a few days.**

Filling:

Preheat oven 200°C/400°F.

Dot over the bottom of the pan:
100 g / 3 oz cold butter
cut into little pieces
and sprinkle this with
100 g / 3 oz sugar.
Peel, quarter and core,
8-12 apples *(Granny Smiths).*
Place a layer of apples core side facing UP on top of the butter pieces and the sprinkled sugar. Press down gently.
Repeat layer of apples core side facing *DOWN*.
Dot these two layers of apples with:
50 g / 1 ½ oz cold butter
cut into little pieces,
50 g / 1 ½ oz sugar
on top.
Put on a medium heat on the stove top until caramelised *(40 minutes).*
Roll one ball of pastry *(doesn't matter if it breaks, just patch it up).*
Cover the apples with the pastry tucking the edges down inside the rim with a spoon handle.
Place in the oven for 20-30 minutes.
Take out when golden and immediately run a knife around the edge.
Put an inverted serving plate on top, turn over, tap the pan, pray, and gently lift off.

Sarah D'Arcy's Secret Tuile

So simple, so good and so impressive. Very good to know how to do if desserts are not your forte - as is my case.

Preheat oven 200°C/400°F.

Buy
puff pastry,
defrost, roll thin using
icing sugar
in the same way that you would use flour.
Starting at one end roll it up tightly like a cigar and wet the edges to seal.
Cut into 1" lengths, stand on end and roll into a circle - very thin.
(Still using icing sugar as you would flour).
Lay the tuiles on a non-stick baking tray and cover with a
roasting rack. *(Yes, I said a roasting rack. You see this stops them from rising).*
Bake in oven until the underside is caramelised,
about 12 minutes.
Take out and cool.
In a blender or a food processor make a coulis of :
sugar,
red berries,
liqueur.
Strain.
Whip
some cream.
On a plate build:
a dollop of cream,
some whole berries,
a tuile,
sprinkling of icing sugar.
Drip coulis around.

Berries with Kirsch and Mint

Ooh!

Mix some berries - I like:
raspberries,
strawberries,
blueberries.
Put them in a serving dish.
Sprinkle with:
1 ½ tbs sugar,
some liqueur e.g.
Kirsch, Triple Sec or Grand Marnier.
Mix it all up gently and chill.
Serve with
some mint leaves
on top.

option:

- **If you want something more substantial tip them into Marks and Spencer's brandy snap baskets.**

Chilled Orange Slices

This is delicious alone or with Crème Brulée *(page 142)* or with Nicole's Chocolate Truffle Cake *(page 154)*.

With a very sharp knife peel and thinly slice
4 oranges.
Place in a shallow serving bowl and add:
peel of 1 lemon grated,
juice of ½ a lemon,
juice of 2 oranges,
5 tbs of sugar.
Turn slices over carefully, cover the bowl and chill, turning when you remember.

note:

- I'll swear I never said this but *DON'T* add any alcohol - much more refreshing without.

Nicole's Chocolate Truffle Cake

This is the most sinful and glorious ending to a dinner that I can think of. I first had it at my friend Nicole's and I can also think of no better way to end this book.

Preheat oven 165°C/325°F.

In a bowl placed over a pot of simmering water, melt:
200 g / 6½ oz of semi-sweet chocolate
200 g / 6½ oz butter.
Cool.

In a mixer *(not a food processor)* beat:
155 g / 5 oz sugar,
4 egg yolks
until thick and lemon coloured.
To this mixture add:
the cool chocolate/butter mixture
and
45 g / 1½ oz flour.

In another mixing bowl beat
4 egg whites
until soft peaks form.
Fold the chocolate mixture into the egg whites and blend well.
Butter and flour
a 9" springform pan and pour in the mixture.
Bake for 30 mins.
DO NOT OVERCOOK! THIS CAKE MUST REMAIN MOIST!
Sprinkle the cake with
icing sugar,
stick a flower in the middle if you are feeling creative and serve either alone or with *Chilled Orange Slices (page 153)* or fresh raspberries.

Index

arborio &

Agnello 90
Anchovies 8
Apple Cider Vinegar 8
Apple Endive & Stilton 84
Aspen Pastini 73
Asparagus 8
Arborio 12
Artichokes 8
Arugula 77 106

balsamic &

Baking 8
Balsamic Vinegar 8
Bean Salad 38
Beef & Capers 105
Beef Stroganoff 108
Berries 152
Borscht 27
Brie 9
Burning 8

chicken &

Carrots 9
Caterers 10
Cheese 9
Chevre 33
Chicken 96
Chocolate Truffle Cake 154
Choucroute 110
Coffee Grounds 9
Consommé 9
Coq au Vin 100
Corn Chaat 81
Courgette 132 136
Crème Brûlée 142
Crème Caramel 140

duck &

Danish Blue 9
Desserts 140 - 154
Dogs Dinner 9
Dried Beans 9
Duck 9 98

eggplant &

Eggs 10 51 57
Eggplant 41 134
Entertaining 10
Entrecôte 108
Escarole 130

fennel &

Fattoush 85
Fennel 83 131
Feta 9
Fish 114 - 120
Flush 10
French Onion Soup 17
Frisée 56
Fruit Soups 144

gratin &

Gazpacho 25
Gorgonzola 9 63
Gratin of Potatoes 124 127
Green Vegetables 10

herbs &

Herbs 10
Hot Oil 11

ikan &

Imperial vs Metric 11
Involtini 35
Gulai Ikan 118

kirsch &

Berries 152

linguine &

Lamb 90 92 94 95
Leeks 39
Lentils 18
Linguine alle Vongole 65
Lobsters 11 120
Lotte 117

marsala &

Mackerel 44
Marsala 146
Melanzane 41 134
Menu Deciding 10
Metric 11
Milk-fed Lamb 92
Mise En Place 11
Monkfish 117
Mozzarella 9

olive oil &

Oil 11
Onion Pie 37
Oregano 11
Oranges 11 152
Oxtail 111

pesto &

Parmigiano 9
Pasta 11 63 - 75
Paté 59
Pesto 67
Pears 146
Persian Yoghurt Soup 22
Place Seating 10
Pot Au Feu 104
Potato 12 124 - 127

rissotto &

Rapini 12
Ray 45
Recipes 12
Red Pepper 33 35
Reducing 12
Re-inventing 12
Rice 12
Roast 90 - 94
Roquefort 9 109
Roquette 77 106

saltimbocca &

Sage 102
Salad 12 81 - 87
Salmon 114
Salt 12
Saltimbocca 102
Sauté 12
Sauces For Fish 114
Sauces For Meat 108 109
Sbollichini 21
Scallops 49
Shopping List 10
Skate 45
Small Talk 12
Soups 17 - 27
Spaghetti 71
Spanish Omelette 31
Squid 43
Starters 31 - 59
Stilton 9
Stock 13
Stirring 12

tarte tatin &

Tagliata 106
Tarte Tatin 148
Thai Beef 55
Tomatoes 13 81 128
Tone 10
Tuile 150
Turnips 98

vitello &

Veal 53 102
Vegetables 124 - 136
Vichyssoise 19
Vongole 65

wine &

Wisdom 8 - 13

zest

For life!
Zucchine 134 136

Santa Kim and her Reindogs

Photograph by Olive Palmer

food

to die for!